Diary of a Damaged Damsel:

Lyrical Life Lessons

By: ShaRhonda "ShayLynn" Sharp

To Whom It May Concern...
This book is dedicated to all of the characters in my life story…the Heroes and the Villains. There is no me without you. God made our bonds necessary.
Peace & Blessings to you all.

Preface

I discovered my love for the written word at a very young age. Creating stories with complex characters and infinite worlds. It wasn't until I got older that I realized my creativity was actually my SOLACE. To pour my pain and passion into the pages was such a powerful and purifying release for me. I've always been that shy, introvert who never really liked to talk about my feelings…mostly out of fear of appearing weak. So my pen and pad became my confidant. My therapeutic relief when this life became a bit too much to deal with.

But, I was told once, "The world needs your voice," and that stuck with me for years. This compilation of poems and random thoughts is my gift to the world—my supplying of the world's needs as requested.

"Diary of a Damaged Damsel" is my story in my words, and I hope it helps you to better understand the girl you once knew and the woman you love today. This is as vulnerable as it gets, people! Enjoy 🖤

Diary of a Damaged Damsel

> *"Keep in mind that I'm an artist, and I'm sensitive about my shit! So, y'all be nice about it. Alright?"*
>
> ---The Queen Mother, Erykah Badu---

Late night musings...

I don't have what it takes to ruin lives the way I want to. I've been dealt some tragic blows and trashy ass hands over these last 30 years. I have all rhyme, reason and rage to wreak havoc on the lives of those who've wronged me. However, I'm such an empath and emotional siphon, that I can never bring myself to purposely inflict pain on someone. I am a Healer.

I take the most broken, battered souls and cut myself to shreds trying to mend them back together. I deplete myself of everything I have, selflessly so, in an effort to fill voids and fulfill lives that are not my own. I am a Healer.

I love the unlovable and unwilling. I remind the most amnesiac spirits that there is insurmountable value in their voice and vastly stretching light left in their smile. I ignite the flame that used to burn brightly within them, but is now barely above a flicker. I touch and change lives and see the beauty beneath the bandages. I am a Healer.

But who is there to heal me?

Diary of a Damaged Damsel

Awkward Silence

You never saved me…
But then again, how could you?
With swallowed words and bitten tongues,
I was the mute to your deafness.
I was the shy one who kept silent.

I saw the look in the eyes of all my fans.
All those so proud of me, including You.
If only folks knew the secrets I harbored,
Then I doubt they would look upon me
With such glowing admiration

You never saved me…
But then again, how could you?
Could you really handle the truth?
Would you believe what I said?
Would you take my side or disown me?
With swallowed words and bitten tongues,
I was the shy one who kept silent.

If I said it was my fault,
would you accept that?
If I said I had to, would that be ok?
If I told you I said "No,"
But nobody listened
Would that be a good excuse?

Time traveling faster than light.
And each day
I bury my secrets deeper within myself
Buried so deep
That they will only resurface from my grave.
You never saved me…
But then again, how could you?

With swallowed words and bitten tongues,
I was the shy one who kept silent.

Would you really want to know?
Know that I thought it was ok…
Know that I let it happen…
Know that I laid still while he didn't…
Know that his breath & sweat were lost
Into every pore of me…

Would you really want to know?
Know that he undressed me hurriedly…
Know that he watched the door for fear
that you would see…
Know that he never looked at me
or even said "Please…"

Would you really want to know?
Know that I kept my secret
not to disappoint you…
Know that I didn't say a word to protect us:
Me from him…
Him from you…
And you from depression…

Know that I felt safe in my self-inflicted
State of Solitude…
Know that my silence has kept me company
For YEARS…

You never saved me!
But then again, maybe I didn't want you to.

Sweet Bitterness

It's a shame, you know?
Living in silence for so long.
It's a shame, you know?
Having nothing but your secrets to keep you company.

It's exhausting, you know?
Smiling through your hidden pain
Because you're the strong one.
It's exhausting, you know?
Living day in and day out with this brick-laden
memory residing on your shoulders.

It's stressful, you know?
Sharing the same space and time with you.
Pretending that our history isn't tarnished
all to be damned.
It's stressful, you know?
Praying for better days,
Wishing for simpler times, and smacking into reality
like a brick wall that refuses to budge.

Bittersweet, they say…
The salt in sugar, they say…
We all have our crosses to bear, they say…
What doesn't kill us makes us stronger, they say…
Smile first, cry later, they say…
Never let them see you sweat, they say…

All I ask is "Why not?"

Why not let them see the damage they've done?
Why not let them know the pain they've caused?
Why not let them be destroyed by the secrets they forced
on me?

Why is their peace of mind more important to me than mine is to them?

Bittersweet, they say…

I say, dance like no one is watching.
I say, cry even when the rain stops
so that your tears take center stage.
I say, scream louder than the thunder.
I say, welcome the questions that follow.
I say, Tell Somebody…

Tell them how beaten and battered your soul is.

Tell them how empty your womb is because of the breaking and entering of your temple.

Tell them how you pray to God
that you were the only one, because you know
that you are strong enough to live with it.

Tell them how much you thank God
that they only had boys.
Because then at least their children are safe with them.
Because you weren't….

Diary of a Damaged Damsel

Mementos

Who remembers their first kiss?

Fumbling movements. Trembling bodies.
Unchoreographed first steps towards intimacy.
Adorable nervousness that tickles your soul
From the inside out.
While you desperately wonder…
"What do I do with my hands?"

Are those the moments frozen in time?
Permanently imprinted on your subconscious
as that long-remembered secret shared humorously, but
silently between those beautiful sets of eyes all your own?

Or is it the way you felt at that moment?
The way your skin flushed red and warm as he leaned in
so close that he made you contemplate whether he should
wait for the invitation…
but, simultaneously you tell yourself
"I wish he would hurry up and put me out of my misery!"

Was it the way butterflies danced a ballet up your spine
as he caressed your face and his fingers made long,
passionate, hungry love to the hair that hung loosely about
your shoulders?

There will always be moments in our lives
that sing constant lullabies to our memory
that we cannot become deaf to.
Was this a moment for you?

Who remembers their first crush?

Flawless skin. Body sculpted from

the hands of God and Michelangelo himself.
Ruby red lips that glistened
every time the sun tip-toed across her glossed mouth.
The way she tilted her head ever-so slightly
when she smiled with her eyes.
Eyes that told the most enticing stories
without her even parting her lips.

Is this the image you paint behind closed lids
as you escape into a dream where you
master the art of seductive conversation
that teases every delicious inch of her ear?

Or is it that one time, on that one day
that you will never forget?
The moment when you mustered up all of your courage and
confidence just to tell her how beautiful you really think
she is?
But then you see HER hand-in-hand with HIM!

He who shall not be named.
He who uses and abuses women occupationally
because there are 24hrs in a day,
7 days in a week,
365 days in a year
and he can't find anything else to do with his time?

He, who along with her, delivers an unwanted,
unwarranted parcel at your feet…
The empty box to deposit the pieces of your heart and
shattered resolve into.

There will always be moments in our lives
that screech like banshees in the night.
Awakening us to the harsh existence where pain is real.

Diary of a Damaged Damsel

So, do we hold tight to that metaphorical
blanket of warm fuzzy memories,
riddled with pretty faces and cute laughs?

Or do we stare at the closed closet door,
awaiting the cardiac arrest that flies out at us
carrying the reminder of your first real emotionally
damaging experience with it?

Who remembers the first time you heard
those soul-stirring words, "I love you?"

As tears welled up in your eyes,
Your voice got so trapped in your throat,
all you could accomplish
was a breathy whisper of reciprocation.

The kiss that followed, and passion that threatened to boil
over and consume the two of you.
Sweeping you off into a rosy abyss.

That defining moment
where you knew more than ever
that your union was real
and built on a rock-solid foundation
held up by emotionally-unstable tectonic plates
that caused aftershocks known as disagreements
that followed behind big arguments, but eventually died
down to become electrifying makeup sex.

Is that your therapeutic way of recalling embedded
memories?

Or do you look in the mirror,
not recognizing the face that you see

because somewhere along the line of building that rock-solid foundation, your identity became buried and lost?
As you touch your black and blue decorated eye socket that has swollen your eyelids shut,
and assess just how much foundation, mascara, eyeshadow and diverting conversation it would take
to not make people stare at you?

Then, do you choose to remember the cause-and-effect chain that wrapped itself around you like a boa constrictor as he emptied that bottle of Jack Daniels and deemed it necessary to introduce his knuckles to your face?

Or do you remember that piss poor apology
swimming in horrible morning breath and endless vomit that he tossed over his shoulder at you this morning?

Do you remember that the first time he said "I love you," it was preceded by his open right hand
coming across your cheek…
causing those tears to well up in your eyes?

Or that his right and left hand coincided with one another to compress your windpipe…
causing your voice to get trapped in your throat
while he demanded that you say those same words back to him…
and all you could manage was a breathy whisper as you struggled to maintain your oxygen supply?

The moments in our life that tend to have
negative elements out-weighing the positive ones,
often leaving us conflicted
on how we should remember those moments.

But who needs long-term memory when you have a constant reminder greeting you every morning disguised as your reflection?

There will always be moments in our lives
that we wish we could have back.

Perhaps to do things over.
Maybe just to relive the joy they brought to our lives.

Or possibly to learn a life lesson that was hidden beneath the surface like asbestos...
ready to damage our lives permanently.

Selective memory isn't healthy.
Remember what you want to make you feel better.
Recall what you need to help you sleep at night.

But the truth will always linger after your cerebral dissection.

And pretty soon the truth will be all you have left.

Scary, isn't it?

Masquerade

I am Drowning…
Stretching and reaching for the surface
Desperately searching for the air that escapes me.

I am Suffocating…
Gasping and choking as my throat closes.
The amnesia within my lungs as I forget how to breathe.

I am Lost…
Treading paths unfamiliar to me.
Revisiting places that once hurt me,
because it is all I know.

I am Longing…
Hoping for a love unrequited.
Dreaming of repeating nightmares.

I am Hopeless…
Asking for the unrealistic.
Demanding the unobtainable.
Getting nothing for my troubles.

I am Desperate…
Accepting less than what I deserve,
just for the sake of saying I have something.

I am Empty…
A hollow vessel riddled with holes.
Trying aimlessly to fill myself with
meaning.

I am the Face of Depression…
No identity to call my own.
Numb to the world around me.

Diary of a Damaged Damsel

The only way I feel is when I hurt me…

Drink until vomit is induced.
Inhale the pills until I am overcome by lethargy.
Allow the jagged blade to dance its mutilating ballet
against my skin.
Love wholly and completely
with the expectation of reciprocation.
A fool's errand, I know.
But, I do it anyway…

I am Dying Slowly…
Of my own doing.
By my own hand.
Fading away into oblivion,
because this life is too much.

BUT, you needn't worry!

I'll still smile
I'll still laugh
I'll still dance and be the life of Life!
Because that's what you need from me.

I will be the puppet on the strings.
I will be the face-painted mime in the invisible box.
I will be the court jester for your entertainment.

Your pearl of wisdom
Your advocate and adversary
Your cheerleader and coach
Your partner in crime.

I will be for you what you are not to me.
I will be for you what you refuse to be for me.

I will be the pretender.
I will be the selfless giver.

I will wear the mask you made for me,
And smile now, cry later…or not at all.

I will do all of this because YOU need me to…

But, I will be dying…
Because I need me to…

Diary of a Damaged Damsel

In the End

Immaculately Imperfect…

There is beauty in my Brokenness.
The depths of my damage are indescribable
My scars exist well-beyond the surface

Vigilant, yet volatile
Desperately discreet
Silently screaming in ample agony.

Miraculously Marred…

My smile is the mask I wear to keep others comfy
My pleasant persona appeasing my audience
Cracking jokes and sing-song sarcasm
Tap-dancing to a tune not my own
Jazz hands and spirit fingers waving joyously in the wind
The Sad Clown…

My story is fraught with despair.

My life is a living nightmare
that I'm fighting to wake up from.
But, fighting alone is exhausting
and asking for help makes me nauseous.

My willingness to depend on others is
non-existent, no matter how deep you dig.

I learned early on that I can't depend on a single soul.
And every chapter of that lesson
came harsher and harsher each time I leveled up.

All I've ever known is to be the "Strong One."

I was never entitled to my own pain.
Ordered to "Suck it up" and never
let people know they got to you.

Problem is, all those buried feelings and swallowed words
start to build up…

No longer remaining bottled up and demanding to be felt,
Emotions are ravenous beasts off the leash.

Fangs dripping with venom
Bloodshot eyes and guttural growls
to narrate the rage ready to spill forth.

Waiting on the first viable prey to show up,
so the Beast can attack.

But when you've isolated yourself with nothing
but your misery to keep you company,
you have no choice but to turn that rage on yourself.

Now, that buried, suppressed, black hole known as
Emotions has no other option
but to swallow you whole just to satiate its appetite.

Dining on despair.
Washing it down with the wine of weariness
Satisfying its sweet tooth with your sadness
You are consumed by your Emotions.

Betrayed by yourself.
Treachery & Treason
Destruction & Devastation
All at the hands of your own mind…
The easiest way to find safety is to remove yourself from
the situation, right?

Diary of a Damaged Damsel

How do you separate and severe ties
with your-DAMN-self?

How do you end your own suffering?
When you figure it out, let me know…

Unrequited Love…That's that BULLSHIT!!

The one thing worse than having your heartbroken by someone you love, is to have it broken by someone who didn't even love you back. We often hear the narrative about "unrequited love," but what is that exactly? Supposedly, it is that instance where you love someone, most often romantically, but they either never acknowledge that love, or they never reciprocate it.

How shitty is that?! You find this person who epitomizes perfection in your eyes. They ooze sex appeal in every way possible. They touch the deepest parts of you without even using their hands. You have no choice but to fall in love with them. Only someone who fits the above description can awaken such a deep yearning in your soul. However, that same Shakespearean-style specimen can destroy your whole outlook on love with one blank stare-laced response to your professing of love.

You practice your speech in the mirror on how you're going to pour your heart out. Testing out facial expressions, hand gestures and fighting back the dramatic tears. Noting different reference points to jog their memory so they can know all of the moments and reasons for why you love them.

And then in return you get…NOTHING!

The heart is a muscle used to pump blood and oxygen through the body. Its purpose is to sustain life. However, much like the brain, memories are imprinted on the heart. You will always be able to relive that moment when you realized you were in love. Unfortunately, you will also always remember the moment when you found out they weren't…

Love Me, Hate Me

My life. My love.
My heart and soul.
My diamond. My pearl.
My silver and gold.
My passionate pretender.
My past, present, and future.
My soul purpose and defender.

Given unto you was my life.
Given unto you was my freedom.
Given unto you was my purity.
Given unto you was my sanity.

Taken from me was my happiness.
Taken from me was my peacefulness.
Taken from me was my love.
Taken from me was my gift to the world.
Taken from me was my chance to be your girl.

Given unto me was anger.
Given unto me was pain.
Given unto me was mind strain.
Given unto me was betrayal.
Given unto me was living hell.

Taken from you…Not a damn thing!

You say one thing,
but mean something totally different.
You are like a sin, and I must repent.
I loved you and swore to never leave.
A lot of good that did me.

I'm sick and I'm tired.

I'm sick of fighting.
I'm tired of crying.
I'm sick of losing sleep.
I'm tired of this shit.

Right now, you have a choice.
God gave you vocals. Use your voice.

Tell me how you feel.
Tell me what's real.
Right now, I want to know.
Where is this going to go?

I demand you to tell me.

Tell me!
TELL ME!
Love me or Hate me
Which one is it?

Diary of a Damaged Damsel

OBLIVION

I wander aimlessly through this life.
No direction or destination to speak of.
And yet, forever and always
I end up at your doorstep.

The concrete melts beneath my feet
as the Earth moves to swallow me whole.
To save me from the agony that awaits me…
The agony that is sure to greet me when I knock.

Trampled tulips and marble-stone decorated paths,
withered and weathered bushes
adorn the door to my fate.
Darkness behind closed doors that beckon me.

I ring the bell…SILENCE.
I knock on tattered screened doors…SILENCE.
Rapping, tapping on grimy window panes…SILENCE.

Starry nights carried by the wind into sunshine morn.
Still, I stand waiting for an answer.
To gain entry into the only asylum I've ever
known…SILENCE.

Where do you go when the asylum won't commit you?

How do you run away with the circus
when the circus doesn't want you?

How do you answer the unanswered questions
when your requests for a moment are ignored?

Who do you ask to save you when don't want to be saved?
SILENCE…

Forbidden Fruit

We both have eyes,
but you will never see me the way I see you.
Your gaze will never behold
such unrelenting beauty and perfection.

You look through me like glass
but can faintly make out a semblance of a silhouette.

I fade into the painted walls you brush past.
Disappear into the trampled carpet beneath your feet.

If I can manage to breathe above a whisper,
then you might hear me serenading the wind
with your name.

I wonder…

Does your reflection make you cry?
Are you moved by the sheer sight of yourself?

The lift in your cheekbones…
The chestnut richness of your eyes…
Your honey-coated lips dripping with sweetness
that tempts even the strongest will to toss caution aside
and greet that sugar rush happily…

The curve of your spine…
That winding road traveling up
from the valley that is resting below your waist
and moves melodically between the boulders you call
shoulders…that call out to me.

I long to touch you but fear that I would set you ablaze with
this burning desire raging inside of me…

Diary of a Damaged Damsel

Nobody's Home

I ran myself through with a blade
Slit myself open and poured out the contents of my soul
into the palms of your hands…

You splayed your fingers and watched as all of me
splashed to the ground.
Seeping into the cracks of the concrete and nothing…

You smeared the remnants of what once was
across your fingers.
As if trying to rid yourself of the burden of my love…

I looked into the black orbs staring blankly back at me
Trying to find some semblance of emotion within the
emptiness…

A second thought?
No.

A twinge of regret?
No.

A flicker of reciprocation?
No.

Nothing.
No.

Nobody came.
Because nobody's home…

Toxic Love: What feels good to you, isn't good for you

What is "Toxic Love?" Toxic Love is that love that comes disguised as the real thing. It feels so damn good. Gives you butterflies in your stomach. Makes your heart race with the slightest touch. It tells you all of the things you want to hear when you want to hear them. It kisses you mid-argument and sex you up to make you forget what you were mad about...or so we think. The important thing to remember about "Toxic Love" are the disguises it wears.

Often times we are so engulfed by the desperation to find and feel love that we ignore the warning signs that would let us know when someone means us no good. Here are a few warning signs to let you recognize "Toxic Love":

- ❖ **What they do**: Make you the scape goat for why they hurt you
    - **What they mean**: "I'm not responsible for the pain you allowed me to cause you."
    - **Why its toxic**: If someone is incapable of apologizing, then they are incapable of seeing the error in their ways. Definition of NARCISSISTIC. They see no wrong in the things they do or say. If anything, their words and actions are a direct result of the freedom they are given to do what the fuck they want. They are not responsible for being courteous, compassionate, respectful...hell, HUMAN! A normally functioning human-being knows right from wrong and fully understands cause and effect; and knowing where to place that blame appropriately. A Toxic Lover has no concept of either, and would rather the one they hurt shoulder the responsibility. To love someone requires you to not only be concerned with their happiness, but to also be responsible in ensuring said happiness. Otherwise, do you really love them?

    - ❖ **What they say**: "I think you're beautiful, but..."
        - **What they mean**: "You need some physical improvements for your imperfections."
        - **Why its toxic**: If someone claims to love you truly, then what that means is that despite all of your faults and flaws, they still see the beauty in you...physically or

otherwise. There shouldn't be a "but" that follows a statement like "You're beautiful," unless it's an equally powerful compliment. To be loved beyond all circumstances is the point of being in love. Anything else is a waste of time.

- ❖ **What they say**: "You need to stop being so paranoid and insecure."
    - **What they mean**: "Stop questioning what I do when I do it and who I do it with."
    - **Why its toxic**: Often times, our gut feelings and intuition may have us looking "paranoid" to others but rarely do we get those feelings without good reason. Even if they are residuals leftover from a past indiscretion that you thought you forgave and forgot about. When they get upset with you for questioning their actions or intentions, what they are telling you is that they don't want to constantly be reminded of their mistakes and/or failures. By them disregarding your festering wounds as paranoia or insecurity is just a not-so-subtle display of their lack-luster interest in a way to repair the damage they've done.

- ❖ **What they do**: They use sex as a band-aid to cover up their misdeeds
    - **What they mean**: As long as you're still willing to have sex with them, then they are still "in good with you."
    - **Why its toxic**: Sex is a means of connection and communication. It is meant to bring a couple closer together in the most intimate way possible. It should never be used to stifle emotions or to "shut you up." It also should never be used as a justification for their poor behavior and your willingness to forgive it. You forgive their transgressions because you love them, care for them and know that they are greater than their decisions. Not because the sex is good! Laying with them is not the equivalent of giving them a "hall pass" to keep fucking up!

Toxic Love

You penetrate me deeply.
Ravishing my resolve
and mauling my mind.
You retreat…and penetrate again.
Plunging deeper…harder…stronger

Twisting…switching positions.
Finding your home in every orifice I have.
And some I didn't know I possessed.
Lying deep inside me.

Engulfing all that surrounds me.

Stripping me bare but making me whole.
Pulling me close
and making me dance to your rhythm.
Inhaling sharply.
Moaning loudly.
Crying sweetly.
Worshipping you
as you invade my soul
Without question or permission

I writhe against you,

You press yourself deeper, still.
I beg for release, but you refuse to let go.

With your intimate kiss against me,
You release the contents of your being
To allow us to become one.

Sweet serenity.
Warm rapture.

Diary of a Damaged Damsel

Delicate desire.
Delicious and decadent.
Purely possessive.

You own me, and I surrender.
My eyes disappear
Into the deep recesses of my mind
My breath is lost between climaxes.

Our whimsical waltz carries us
to a cloud, where we float
for an infinity.

To love you is to lose me.
But I find refuge in your toxicity

Oh, Heroin!
How I love thee…

Ode to Destruction

Pick your poison…
But choose wisely.
For it will be the cause of your destruction.
Do not use a conqueror's mind
or a warrior's spirit when you choose.
There is no saving you.
The end is inevitable.

Destruction by Drink…
Smooth pouring over jagged cubes.
Sift and swish to enhance its effects.
Sip slow to gage its potency.
Rush the gulp to quicken the overtaking.
And then…wait.

Destruction by Drug…
Snort. Sniff. Taste. Take.
Smoke. Swallow. Inhale. Ingest.
Invite this volatile vigilante
To find refuge in your spirit.
Become consumed. Be engulfed.
And then…wait.

Destruction by Design…
Dye your hair. Botox your brows.
Inflate your lips, hips and nips.
Shave. Strip. Wax. Weigh.
Again and again…
Detox your body of your soul.
Become the new you.
And then…wait.

Destruction by Devotion…
The quickest, easiest of the vices.

Diary of a Damaged Damsel

The most effective path to destruction.
The all-consuming, devouring.
Most destructive end of all endings.
No waiting or wanting.
No timeless torture.
All you have to do is…
Love.

Late Night Musings…

"Tis better to have loved and lost than to never have loved at all."

Whoever said that is full of shit! To love and be loved is one of life's greatest gifts. That burst of raw joy you feel from deep within. Finding the other half of your heart & soul walking around in human form is indescribable. Sadly, so many people go through life never knowing what that's like. And when you do have it, things tend to feel so much better. But when you lose it…BABY!!

Talk about your world falling apart. The immeasurable emptiness you're left with. You feel robbed and cheated out of the lifetime you were promised and prayed for. Watching their love story unfold right before our eyes these last few weeks, my heart breaks for Lauren London because she has to raise her children telling them about this wonderful man they'll never get to meet. She has to navigate through life now while not being done loving her man, but also never being able to hear him say "I love you, too" ever again.

MY….GOD!!!

Rest in Peace,
Ermias "Nipsey Hussle" Asghedom
8/15/85 - Infinity
The Marathon continues…

Diary of a Damaged Damsel

Forever Ain't Feeble

I'd shatter myself into pieces
Sprinkle the shards into the wind
Just hoping that at least part of me
Will end up where you are.

I'd shed my skin
Strip myself bare of all that is my own
Just to give you a blank canvas
To mold me into the woman you need.

I'd divulge all of my secrets
Pour out my heart until the cup runneth over
Just to make room for you
To make me your diary of discretion
Your temple of trust

I'd stop my heart for you
Hold my breath until it is lost within me
Just so that you can be the one to breathe life into me
To save me from myself…like I need you to

I'd dance for you…
I'd sing for you…
I'd cry for you…
I'd live for you, because dying would be too easy…

I'd move for you…
I'd sit still for you…
I'd stop time for you…
I'd wait for you…

To be wanted by someone is too simple.
Need me…
Crave me…

Yearn for me…
Devote yourself to me…

Let me be the idol you pray to…
Let me be the church that you pray in…
Let me be the waters you cleanse yourself in…
Let me be the wind that embraces you daily…
Let me be all you need and need not for anything else…

All I ask for in return is that you be my sanctuary…
The peace and comfort that I've sought for so long.

Please, be real and actual.
For, suffering heartbreak at the hands of my imagination is not the route I wish to take.

Be my happy place…
Be my Neverland…
Be my Never-ending Story that I can't stop telling…

Diary of a Damaged Damsel

Defiance

I died in your arms last night…
Well, not exactly.
I died wrapped in my arms, imagined as yours.
You counted my breaths.
Hanging on edge to see which one would be the last.

I inhale sharply.
My chest rising heavenward.
I exhaled slowly, my breath kissing yours.
And then…I lived.

I sat erect on the floor.
Looking about me to discern where I was.
I stood slowly, finding my balance I'd lost in the hardwood.
Stumbling Frankenstein-esque through the room.
I let those 40 watts invade the darkness.
Adjusting my eyes to its brightness.
And then…I lived.

I shuffled through this home I had to make without you.
I inhaled again,
but the weight of it was crushing.
Like bricks burying me with grief and rage.
I exhaled in the form of tears and screams.
I inhaled again…exhaled again…
And then…I lived.

The NERVE!

Continue on when that wasn't the plan?
The NERVE!
You lit the fire and walked away.
You crashed the car into the tree and walked away.
You rolled my body down the steep side of a hill

into a forgettable ditch and walked away.
And I lived…

The NERVE!

No hospital rooms for us.
But in the comfort of our own bed, wrapped in a quilt I hand-stitched for you 80 years from now…
Surrounded by children, grandchildren, great-grandchildren, and dear friends who all have out lived us…

I was supposed to die with you!
Not at the hands of you.
This is not my idea of romantic.

So, I lived…
The NERVE!

I found my breath.
I found my smile.
I found my joy.
I found me buried in that shallow grave you thought would do the trick.

You walked away.
I let you.
You chose otherwise.
I let you.
You forgot me.
And I lived!

Without you, I lived.
The nerve…

You left me to die in a puddle of tears.

Diary of a Damaged Damsel

Surrounded by nothing but my memories left to memorialize a life poorly lived.

But I got up.
I wiped those tears.
I breathed easy.
I lived…

The NERVE!!!
You're welcome.

Late Night Musings…
♪♪ *If all it is is eight letters, why is it so hard to say?* ♪♪

  We talk frequently and openly about the most complex things…meaning of life, is the sky really blue, immigrating back to Africa and all that kinda shit. I can pour out all the ugliest parts of my soul in the palms of your hands and you don't even flinch.
  I tell you my hopes…dreams…and darkest nightmares. Even when I try so desperately to hide behind façades and reinforced defense mechanisms, my camouflage is no match for your x-ray vision into the depths of my soul. Whatever I vocalize you support it with the shoulders of a god.

  I speak life into you without taking a breath and you do the same for me. I smile and laugh at the slightest suggestion from you. I invite you into my temple without hesitation. We worship at each other's alters until the minutes tick into hours.

  Touching…tracing…tempting…tasting until nothing is left and we're still unsatiated because we know there's more. I can scream your name into the void as it travels on the tail of a shattering orgasm and feel ZERO shame about who hears me.

  But, I can't tell you that "I love you," because that would be too weird. That would make things awkward and uncomfortable. That would be crossing boundaries that we both agreed were a necessity to have. So, for the benefit of your comfort, I'll continue to swallow my words.

  Words that try to claw their way out of my mouth every time I say your name. Words that shred the back of my throat like shards of glass. I'll let the agony of my forced silence keep me company because to say how I feel would be wrong…

  ♪♪ *If all it is is eight letters, why is it so hard to say?* ♪♪

A Song of You

I'd write your name
On every blade of grass
Direct a chorus of the North winds
Just to make the Earth sing
A song of you.

My eyes would search the sky
Find the deepest void
in the blackened distance
Inhale deeply and deliver your name into it
Just to make the galaxies echo with
A song of you.

My heart could contract at the thought…
My soul could stir restlessly…
My ears could fall deaf to the world…
My mouth could mute forever…
And yet and still I would sing
A song of you.

Life. Love. Death.
The beginning. The climax. The end.
Lyrics. Melody. Music.
Breaths. Words. Touches.
A poem. A limerick. A haiku.
It's all beautiful.
But the sweetest of all is the song…
The Song of You.

{Untitled}

Like a cloudless sunrise
Bursts of orange and haze
Ascending from nowhere and spreading light everywhere,
Dawning of anew
Signaling the start
Fruitful first chances or infinite second ones
The brightest star in God's sky kisses me every morning.
Like I wish you would…

Spreading like a feather soft blanket
Across the earth's ceiling
Shifting rapidly from pristine white to ominous gray
Swaddling and swallowing up the light of day
Rumbles of thunder and cracks of lightening
The troupe of raindrops tap-dancing against the window pane…
A stormy symphony playing in the background…
But, I have no one to dance with…

Clear skies painted violet and crimson
The sun slipping into something a bit more sensual.
Enticing the moon to come out and play
Slowly lighting the wicks of Galileo's candles.

They flicker against the *blackdrop*.
Cascading constellations in shapely wonders
as far as the eye can see.
The expanse of darkness blots out any traces
of what once was.
A sign of the romantic revolution of the Sun and the Moon
chasing each other but never catching.
Except for ecliptic chance encounters where they brush
past, just close enough but never truly touching.
A never-ending, unsatiated longing…

Diary of a Damaged Damsel

Two ships in the night calling out across the waves just to let each know they're not alone…

To know what you want is right there
And that "right there" is still too far…

So, I'll curl up in the moonlight,
Letting it drape over and caress me through the night until it slips away…

Leaving me alone…like you did…

Shade

Without thought, rhyme or reason
I found my kindred spirit
My Twin Soul during Gemini season
Walking idly by and I didn't know it.

Smiling and laughing all carefree
Shaking hands and kissing babies
All the while, wearing me THIN, simultaneously!
Watching him, and thinking "Hmmm, maybe…"

God put a face on my Twin Soul
Brown, bearded and beautiful with lips like honey and a smile of gold.
Exuding melanin-laced masculinity of the purest kind.
Non-toxic, gentle and so goddamn FINE!

Remaining a stranger who incited my curiosity,
Yet everything about him felt so familiar to me.
Did we worship the holiness of each other in another life?
What level of kinship did we have?
I pray husband and wife…

With a laugh like music,
Smooth jazz on a Sunday morning
Wisdom beyond his years
gives way to conversations that are never boring.

His kiss paints colors on my body I never knew existed.
His hands tracing the story of our life from my top to bottom.
Whispers of what is, what was and what will be caress my lobes…frontal and ear.

And now…we're here…

Diary of a Damaged Damsel

Days, weeks, months and years later

Still dancing an infinite waltz around our feelings.
Never truly knowing what we could be.
Still bound together by our ties...
Ties that unravel every time we touch, because we are each other's undoing...

The thread count in those sheets are no match for you and me
Silver linings in storm clouds
Glitter and glisten less and less
Fairy tales tell of straw spun into gold
But the story of our diamond ties has yet to be told.

Hearts beating in time like Brazilian bongos
Twins twisting and turning to our own Tango.
Nobody hears it, but the pull is magnetic
Eyes watch, intrigued and jealous
Not understanding what this is between us.

My Twin Soul who gets me...
My Kindred Spirit who understands me...
My Polar Opposite who is drawn to me,
and yet continuously pulls away from me...

I wonder, is this bond one-sided?
Is it a seesaw only weighed down on my end?
Was it not revealed to you that our spirits are kindred?
I assure you, I am not meant to only be your friend

When you hurt, I ache
When you cry, I drown in tears
When you feel lost and unworthy, my pain is UNREAL!
When you feel happy, I'm happy for you

When you feel proud, I'm proud of you
When you need me, nothing but death can keep me from showing up.
Moving heaven and earth to be there for you

Giving you all I have and scraping the bottom of the barrel to revive the remnants
Just to be sure you get all you need

I love you so much it hurts…
It hurts to be away from you
Hurts to not hear from you
Hurts when I try to ween myself off you

Have you ever tried shedding your own skin?
Peeling off every layer
Whether slow and steady
or rapid and reckless
The agony is the same.

Stitched together like Siamese siblings
Physically fused from one to the other
To not see you when they see me is impossible.
My mood mirrors yours
Or miseries love company but only if it's us
We are tastefully toxic to each other

But, bittersweet is my favorite flavor…

Diary of a Damaged Damsel

Lifeline

On a chilly, fall day in November '88,
I decided I'd had enough!
See, I was born 6wks ahead of schedule because
I don't like being told what to do or when to do it.

Problem is, my impatience and reckless abandon
for "appropriate" timing cost me
6wks in the NICU with tubes in my nose,
constant medical monitoring
and worrying my mother to death like post-partum mood
swings weren't doing enough damage.

But look at me now! I'm good!!

Fast forward 2yrs and you'll find me
sitting in a doctor's office crying tears of excruciating pain
while Mama Bear demands somebody tell her what's
wrong with her baby's face.

See, I was a medical anomaly
because I was the first documented case of Shingles
on a toddler in medical history.
Go to Rush Hospital and ask about the Kid!

But look at me now! I'm good!!

Even got some cute lil' scars on my face that often get
mistaken for a birthmark…
That's how I get 'em (wink, wink)

Now here's where it gets gritty…

By 9yrs old, I'd lost my innocence.
No…let me rephrase…it was stolen.

Nah, he didn't break the seal
But he forced me to know a man way earlier than I wanted to.

In those moments, yes there were multiple,
I learned in the ugliest way what it meant to be used, abused and ashamed,
but still more concerned with his well-being above my own.

Crazy, right?

By 13yrs old, I learned what it felt like to have my heart broken by the one person I wanted soooo badly to love me…
My ONLY brother forgot my birthday.
The tears were infinite…

By 16yrs old, I experienced "real love" for the first time.

By 17yrs old, it was over.
Her took my self-worth, heart and virginity with him.

By 18yrs old, I had been cheated on and when I tell you EVERYBODY knew about it and not a soul told me SHIT?!

NIGGA!!!

By 22yrs old, I found out that puppy love, heartbreak in high school was like comparing a papercut to a bullet wound.

The Pain…

Diary of a Damaged Damsel

The gut-wrenching, soul-crushing,
literal shattering of your heart
that you can feel as it happens.
That moment where you feel like "If I died right now, I'd be okay with it."
That kind of hurt that has you eyeing sharp objects like you never have before.
How the hell am I expected to survive this?!
The PAIN…

By 25yrs old, all the pain of my past decided it no longer wanted to be suppressed, and hit me like a MACK truck!
Oh, but it's sadistic with it.
Waits good until I'm in a content place in my life and then BOOM!

Tons of bricks of bullshit, depression, anxiety, fantasies of self-harm all smacking me in the face
over and over for days
until it gets bored and then leaves.
Gives me a few days reprieve
And then comes bursting back in like Jack Nicholson in the "Shining" screaming "Here's Johnny!"

By 29yrs old, I'd given my Demons more ammo to use against me in the span of 4 months:

One guy, fooled around with the one bitch I repeatedly asked him about and he gave me the "I don't even feel that way about her" speech.
Worst part? She was a homie.
2 friendships ruined all to hell.

Second guy, violated me by not comprehending that "Stop" and "No" are complete fucking sentences!

Worst part? It happened in my own home.
Ain't enough sage burning in the world for that…

By 30yrs old, I realized I have no idea who I am without my Trauma.
I've never had a moment in my life that didn't end with me damaged and in pain.

I am broken and battle-worn with scars you can see and ones you can't

My life is a testimonial of all the shit NOT to do!
Save yourself from those sacrificial situations.
Avoid where at all possible because what awaits on the other side is supremely less than glamorous.

But you know what else?
My life is also a testimonial of Consistency.
From birth til now, my entire existence has been fraught with one traumatic, life-altering event after another.

I was born with a death sentence attached to my name, but I survived.
My immune system is trash, but I survived.
I was molested, raped, violated, robbed or whatever you wanna call it, but I survived.

I have had an internal,
unspoken love-affair with self-harm
because I would give anything to make this pain stop!

But you know what keeps me here?

It's not my family.
It's not my friends.
It's not the fickle outpouring of love and adoration.

Diary of a Damaged Damsel

You know what it is?

It's because throughout EVERYTHING,
what would be most folks' reason to checkout,
my life still holds value to ME!

I still matter to ME!
I still have living to do for ME!
For all I have suffered, I know there is a greater reward waiting for me.
I can't get it if I'm not here!

I thank God I was born with an impatient and stubborn nature.
I hate being told what to do.

And you think I'm going to let your fucked-up ways dictate when my time is up?

BRUH!!

Dear Future Husband (Disclaimer #2)

Dear Future Husband,

I have prepared a place for you
I have made a space for you
I have prayed for you
I am waiting for you…

I have asked God to mold me
I have asked God to heal me
I have asked God to comfort me
For you, I have asked God to do this in me
Because it is what you deserve

Darlin', it is a privilege to be loved by me
The mountains I will move for you
The things I'll show you that you never dreamed.
All these gifts and wonders solely just for you.

But, we have to clear some things up first.
Address the proverbial elephant…just in case.
Trust me, tis better to speak now
than to have to leave you resting in peace
or pieces…
Because, LOOK HERE!!

So, here goes…(deep breath)

Dear Future Husband,

I love you, already
Chance meetings aren't necessary
I know what your heartbeat sounds like, already
I am all that you need
Trust me!

Diary of a Damaged Damsel

BUT, if you are hell bent & intent
on entertaining your throng of fans and hangers-on,
Lemme 'lone!

If you are hell bent & intent on playing games and being
unsure of what you want,
Lemme 'lone!

If you would rather not be bothered and bogged down
with the necessary requirements & responsibilities of
loving a good woman,
Cool!
But, lemme 'lone!

I am not pressuring a grown man to do a damn thing!

If you are hell bent & intent on increasing your body count
by summer's end,
May the odds be ever in your favor, Luv.
But, lemme 'lone!

You can trust and believe
That I will not, under any circumstances,
ruin or hinder your desires and dreams
to be a Fuck Nigga
Live your best life, Boo!
But lemme 'lone!

I am one hurt feeling away from a homicide
My last nerve is worn so thin
It's damn near transparent

I've got one gray hair per heartbreak
And Dark-n-Lovely ain't working no more!
"Tired" barely scratches the surface

of my exhaustion with the male population.
I curse my adoration and obsession with y'all,
but I'm holding out hope.
Don't ask me why (eye roll)

I have spent more time
with Toni Braxton, Kelly Price and ID TV
than I am certain is healthy.
I will serenade the hell outta the night air
While digging a hole for you
In ya mama's backyard
Because I blame her for your fuckery!

I will Bernie from Waiting to Exhale
The shit outta ya whole life
And handcuff my-damn-self
When the cops show up and scream
"Yeah I did it!" from their backseat
Because FUCK YOU, BRO!

Left Eye, Queen Latifah & Trina raised me
Meaning, I ain't too proud to punch you dead in ya eye and
remind you that You don't know nan!

My love is too precious a thing to be toyed with
That priceless pearl you find in the bottom of the ocean
That delicate flower with fragile petals
That fine china you only bring out on special occasions.

Diamonds, gold, silver, platinum
All fade in comparison to the love
I have in store for you.

Priceless yet valuable.
A gift like no other.

Diary of a Damaged Damsel

My love is like water…
I can cleanse you, quench you and complete you.
But, if you test these waters, one wrong ripple
and the flood that comes,
not even Noah could save you.

Hell hath no fury,
and I ain't got time!
So, stop playing with me, man!

If you mean me no good,
then LEMME 'LONE!

Love you ♥!

Late night musings...

I am many things...PITIFUL is not one of them! My triumphs over my traumas are all the proof I need of that. My ability to keep smiling in spite of all that has happened to me. My strength to pull myself up out of the ditch every time I was left for "dead." My defiance against defeat is deafening to my naysayers. My unwillingness, relentlessness, unmoved and uncompromised nature. My laugh that tickles my ears even still. My faith and belief in the fact that all things are possible. My unshakeable desire to love and be loved, and my drive to achieve just that. My Warrior's Will to protect those dear to me. My honesty about who and what I am. No, I am not pitiful at all. I AM POWERFUL! ♥